NO SUGAR
NO FLOUR
COOKBOOK
WEIGHED & MEASURED MEALS
FOR FAST WEIGHT LOSS

By Jennifer Bismack

My Story

My weightloss journey began after I was misdiagnosed for ADD and the Adderall I was given caused a chemical imbalance in my brain. I normally weighed 130 pounds at 5'2". In order to rebalance my brain I had to take antipsychotics, which caused me to gain 50 pounds in just over one month. diagnosed with a chemical imbalance in my brain.

After trying every diet out there nothing worked for me except for a food plan given to me in a food addict support group. Sure I could loose a couple pounds here and there but nothing compare to my food plan and there was nothing out there I could stick to but the food plan described in this book. I tweaked the plan given to me a little bit to fit my lifestyle and thankfully, I still lost a half a pound per day. In my first 30 days of sticking to the food plan in this book I lost 15 pounds and I am still losing everyday I eat the foods in this cookbook. I started the food plan at 183 and my last weigh in was at 167. I still got 34 more pounds to loose but I was so excited about my weight-loss I had to write this book to help others in their journey as well. Please follow me on my Facebook page "No Sugar No Flour Cookbook & Meal Delivery" to follow me in my journey but, also as a way to come together with others for support.

Expect Weight Loss!

This book is intended to help you lose up to 90 pounds in 90days while averaging a pound a day in weight loss if sticking to the "Rules for your first 90days" food plan. After your first 90 days we will introduce other foods back into your diet to help you maintain your weight loss or you can continue with the food plan in this book to continue to lose weight.

Rules for your first 90days:

No sugar, no flour, no wheat. No Nuts, no dried or dehydrated food, No sugar-unless it is the 5th ingredient or higher in the ingredients list of your dressings, oils, or vinaigrettes, No artificial sweeteners or natural sweeteners except for the sugar that comes in food naturally like in fruits and vegetables, sauces made out of vegetables need to be counted as your cooked vegetable for example tomato or marinara sauce. No potatoes and stay away from starchy vegetables. No ketchup due to the high fructose corn syrup. No rice. When having banana as a fruit never eat more than half of a banana.

For daily healthy fats (4 table spoons a day) you can use oils and salad dressings or vinaigrettes with sugar in it so long as sugar is the 5th ingredient or higher on the ingredients list. You may use mayo but not miracle whip.
If you use Vinegar or Vinaigrettes you can have up to 4 tablespoons on top of your dressing if there is no sugar in it. You are only allowed 3 meals a day and must eat every 4-6 hours with no snacks. Do not skip meals or split meals.

When prepping meals with your protein source cook your protein source separately from your cooked veggies or salad. This way you can measure your vegetable/s and meat separately. For meals that call for meat and beans count your beans /peas as a vegetable and let your cooked vegetable and beans count as one. Meaning don't measure more than 6-oz. of veggies and beans combined.

You can drink, water, coffee, tea, 4oz. of diet soda per day or 4 oz. of crystal light. No milk of any kind may be added to your coffee or tea. No fruit juices allowed.

Do not taste food while cooking, do not watch television, or play on the computer why you eat. Your cravings for sweets and sugars will decline the longer you go without sugar.

What to do if you hit a plateau?
Reduce the number of meals with spices and Stevia.
Limit the # of Yogurt and Fruit Smoothies you consume to 1 per week.
Reduce the amount of oil you use to 1 tablespoon.

Breakfast

For breakfast you always get 6 ounces of fruit. This can be mixed fruit or one type of fruit of your choice. You may also use 2 packets or teaspoons from the natural sweetener Stevia but no other sweeteners or artificial sweeteners are allowed.

You also get ONE of the following in the list below:
2 eggs
2 ounces of cheese
4 ounces of cottage cheese
4 ounces of meat of your choice
4 ounces of tofu
6 ounces of beans or peas
8 ounces of plain yogurt
8 ounces of milk

6-oz. of Watermelon & 4-oz. of Cottage Cheese

2 Eggs with 6-oz. of mixed fruit which include: peaches, a banana, and blueberries.

Breakfast

Frozen Berry Smoothie: 6-oz. of frozen berries, 8-oz. of plain yogurt, 5 ice cubes, and 2 teaspoons of Stevia.

3 and ½ of Bob Evan's Breakfast Sausage Links and 6-oz. of fruit

2-oz. of cheese and 6-oz of fruit

Breakfast

6-oz. of avocado and 2 eggs

6-oz. of Refried Beans and 2 Eggs

6-oz. Pineapples and 4-oz. of
Cottage Cheese

Breakfast

8-oz. Plain Yogurt Mixed with
6-oz. Bananas . Place in a small
paper cup with a toothpick or
popsicle stick and freeze.

6-oz. Baked Cinnamon & Apples with 8-oz. of Yogurt

2-3 TBL ghee or coconut oil3 apples, peeled and cut into small chunks2 tsp. cinnamon1 tsp. nutmegDash of unrefined sea salt¾ – 1 cup filtered water

In a medium sauté pan (with lid), over medium high heat, melt ghee or coconut oil. Add apples and stir to coat with ghee/oil. Add cinnamon, nutmeg and dash of salt. Stir to coat well. Allow apples to cook for a minute or two, until pan is quite hot. Add water (start with ¾ cup) and cover immediately (you want to trap the steam).

Reduce heat to low and allow apples to cook for about 45 minutes, until soft enough to smash with the back of a spoon. Keep an eye on the pan during cooking, and add additional water if needed to keep the pan from cooking dry. The apples should be moist, but not swimming. When soft, smash all the apples to desired consistency and stir well. Can thin with additional water if desired.

6-oz. of Mixed Berries with 8-oz.
of Yogurt.

Breakfast

Combine 2 eggs with 6-oz of bananas blend with blender then fry on stove just like a pancake. No syrup needed!

Sauce & Spice Tips

To give your breakfast food some added flavor try adding any of the following:

- Lemon juice
- Cinnamon
- All Spice
- Hot Sauce
- Vinegar
- Salt or Pepper
- Other Spices

Lunch & Dinner

For lunch and dinner you always get 6 ounces of cooked vegetables. You also get a 6 oz. salad. The salad can be 6 oz. of lettuce, spinach, or mixed greens or it can be a combination of raw vegetables mixed with the lettuce, spinach, or mixed greens as long as the total of the salad equals 6 ounces.

You also get 1 ½ tablespoon of a healthy fat or dressing that includes a fat such as oil. The dressing can have sugar or artificial sweeteners in it as long as it is the 5th ingredient on the list or higher.

You also get ONE of the following in the list below:

2 eggs
2 ounces of cheese
4 ounces of cottage cheese
4 ounces of meat of your choice
4 ounces of tofu
6 ounces of beans or peas
8 ounces of plain yogurt
8 ounces of milk

Lunch & Dinner

Enjoy the Next Pages Which Include Weight loss Recipes from Around the World!

Americana

Asian

Indian

Italian

Greek

Mexican

Cuban

Moroccan

Mediterranean

Australian

Americana

Turkey & Bean Chili Crockpot

Cook 1 pack of Ground Turkey and set aside. Let cool.
Weigh out as many 4-oz. zip lock bags of turkey meat that you can get out of your pack of ground turkey.

Combine the remaining ingredients into a crockpot:
1 cup of chopped red onion
1/3 cup of a chopped poblano pepper
1 teaspoon of minced garlic
1 tablespoon of chili powder
2 tablespoon of tomato paste
2 teaspoon of dried oregano
1 teaspoon of ground cumin
¼ teaspoon of salt
¼ teaspoon of black pepper
1 can of cannellini beans rinsed and drained
1 (14.50oz.) can of diced tomatoes undrained
1 (14-oz.) can of chicken broth
½ cup of cilantro
6 lime wedges

Americana

Turkey & Bean Chili Crockpot

Serve with your favorite salad

Americana

Sauerkraut Carrots, Onions, and Sausage

Cook a pound of sausage separately for best results use kielbasa. Once finished cooking add in 4.-oz of sausage with each meal.

Scoop out 6-oz of cooked vegetables for each meal out of your crockpot.

What to put in the crockpot:

5 cups of chicken stock
1 pack or pound of sauerkraut drained
2 cups of fresh mushrooms sliced
2 large carrots sliced
3 sliced celery stalks
1 chopped sweet onion
1 can diced tomatoes
2 teaspoons of dried dill
pinch of caraway seeds
salt and pepper to taste

Cook on high in crockpot for 5-6 hours

(optional)
Add potatoes after you hit your goal

Lunch & Dinner
Americana

Sauerkraut Carrots, Onions, and Sausage

Serve with your favorite Salad

Diet Soup

1 medium head of cabbage chopped
1 onion, chopped
3 large carrots, chopped
3 celery stocks, chopped
3 tomatoes, chopped
16 ounces of frozen green beans
2 ounces of dry onion soup mix
6 cups of water

Combine water, soup mix and vegetables in a large tock pot and bring to a boil. Reduce heat and simmer until vegetables are tender.

Americana

Diet Soup

Serve with your favorite protein

Roasted Tomato Soup

5 tomatoes, cored (if necessary) and quartered
1 large red bell pepper, seeded and quartered
3 medium yellow onions, peeled, quartered
4 tablespoons extra-virgin olive oil
 5 plump cloves of garlic,
  As needed sea salt
2 - 3 cups light vegetable stock or water
1/4 teaspoon smoked paprika

Preheat the oven to 375F degrees and position 2 racks in the middle of the oven. Line 2 rimmed baking sheets with parchment paper, alternately you can just rub them down with a thin glaze of olive oil.

Arrange the tomatoes, skin side down, on a baking sheet. Coat the bell pepper and onions with olive oil and put them on the other baking sheet along with the garlic, place the pepper skin side down as well. Give both sheets a light showering of salt, then bake until the tomatoes start to collapse and the onions start to brown and caramelize, about 45 minutes. Turn the onions if they start getting overly dark on the bottom. Check on the garlic as well, once the cloves are golden and oozy inside, pull them from the oven.

Peel the garlic, dump all of the roasted vegetables into a big, high-sided bowl, and puree with a hand blender. Alternately, use a conventional blender or food processor and work in batches. Blend in a cup of the stock, and keep adding the rest 1/2 cup at a time until the soup is the desired consistency. I like a little chunk and texture to this soup particularly if the weather has a bit of a chill, but smooth or chunky is your call. Add the paprika and a bit more salt if needed - adjusting to your taste.

Serves 4.

Americana

Roasted Tomato Soup

Serve with your favorite protein

Americana

Best Tasting Meatless Bean Burger

1 can of black beans
1 tablespoon of garlic powder
1 tablespoon of onion powder
2 tablespoons of parsley
1 teaspoon of chili powder
1 teaspoon of cumin
1 teaspoon of oregano
Add a dash of salt and pepper

Mix all ingredients together until you get the texture of raw hamburger meat. For best results blend with a hand held blender or food processor.

Shape into 6-oz. meatless hamburger patties then fry on stove like a burger.

After you have reached your goal weight you can add 1 cup of oats to your bean mixture.

Lunch & Dinner
Americana

Best Tasting Meatless Bean Burger

Serve with your favorite cooked Vegetable & Salad

Americana

Jennifer's Roast Beef Salad

4-oz. deli freshly sliced roast beef (not packaged)
2-oz. mixed greens
4-oz mix of bell peppers, onions, and mushrooms

Sauté 4-oz. veggie mix and roast beef in 1 tablespoon of Kenzoil or your favorite blend of oil and spices for about 3-5minutes.
Once finished cooking pour on top of salad and drizzle on ½ tablespoon of my Homemade Berry Dressing.

Americana

Jennifer's Roast Beef Salad

Serve with your favorite cooked vegetable

Americana

Chicken & Cilantro Lime Pesto Over Zucchini Noodles

To Make Pesto sauce
(Fry 1 Tablespoon and a half with each 6-oz serving of zucchini noodles)

4-oz. of cilantro
½ cup cashews, lightly roasted
2 avocados, peeled and pitted
2 Tablespoons avocado oil or olive oil
2 Teaspoons sea salt
4 cloves of garlic minced, measuring 1 Tablespoon
    (Fry 1 Tablespoon & ½ with each 6-oz serving of zucchini noodles)

Zucchini Noodles with Tomatoes
    Weigh 6-oz. of cherry tomatoes cut in half and zucchini noodles and fry with measured pesto sauce.

Lunch & Dinner
Americana

Chicken & Cilantro Lime Pesto Over Zucchini Noodles
Serve with your favorite salad

Americana

Ham & Split Pea Soup

Cook 4-oz of ham with each 6-oz. of soup

1-16-oz bag of split peas
2-medium carrots chopped
1 small onion chopped
1 large ham bone
½ Tablespoon of black pepper

*Add water if soup becomes to thick
*Add one large potato after you have reached your weight-loss goals

Americana

Ham & Split Pea Soup

Serve with your favorite salad

Americana

Stuffed Peppers

Use 1+ 1/2 pounds sweet Italian sausages or ground turkey and weigh out 4-oz of meat for each pepper.

    1+1/2 cups coarsely grated zucchini (about 1 large)

    1/2 cup finely chopped red onion

    1/3 cup minced fresh parsley

    1/4 cup fine dry breadcrumbs

    1 large egg

    1 teaspoon ground black pepper

    3/4 teaspoon salt

    1/2 teaspoon minced fresh rosemary

    6 small to medium-size red bell peppers, tops removed and   seeded.

Serves 6.

Americana

Stuffed Peppers

Serve with your favorite salad

Americana

Carrot Ginger Soup

1 tablespoon of sweet cream butter
1 onions, peeled and chopped
3 cups chicken broth
1 pounds carrots, peeled and sliced
1 tablespoons grated fresh ginger
1/2 cup whipping cream
Salt and white pepper
Sour cream
Parsley sprigs, for garnish
Dash of garlic powder with each serving

Boil carrots in a large pot until soft then throw all ingredients together into a blender.
Once, pureed put back on stove with no water.

*Garnish with parsley if you reached your goal weight add in cubed breakfast potatoes.

Americana

Carrot Ginger Soup

Americana

Skillet Chicken w/Cherry Tomato's and Garlic

6 (4-oz.) skinless boneless chicken breasts
1 teaspoon of salt
¼ teaspoon black pepper
1 tablespoon of olive oil
2 pints of red and orange cherry tomatoes
3 large garlic cloves finely chopped
3 tablespoons of cider vinegar
2 tablespoons of water
2 tablespoons of fresh parsley

1. Sprinkle both sides of each breast with 1/2 tsp. salt and 1/4 tsp. pepper. Spray large nonstick skillet with cooking spray and set over medium heat. Add chicken and cook until cooked through, 6-7 minutes per side. Transfer chicken to platter. Cover loosely with foil and keep warm.

2. Heat oil in skillet over medium high heat. Add tomatoes and garlic, cook, stirring, until tomatoes are lightly browned, about 2 minutes. Add vinegar, water, parsley, and remaining salt and pepper. Cook until flavors are blended, about 1 minute. Pour tomatoes over chicken.

Serves 6

Lunch & Dinner
Americana

Skillet Chicken w/Cherry Tomato's and Garlic
Serve with your favorite cooked Vegetable & Salad

Americana

Tarragon Thyme Chicken

Serve with your favorite cooked Vegetable & Salad

Spray your pan with coconut oil
Use 3 (4-oz.) boneless chicken breasts
½ tablespoon dried tarragon
½ tablespoon dried thyme
1-teaspoon salt
1-teaspoon black pepper
1 teaspoon dried basil
2 table spoon of minced garlic
3 large lemon slice

Preheat oven to 350 degrees. Coat a medium sized baking dish with cooking spray, Place chicken in small bowl and roll over seasoning, Top with lemon slices and bake for 40 minutes , or until done.

Tarragon Thyme Chicken

Serve with your favorite cooked Vegetable & Salad

Americana

Saffron Chicken

6-(4-oz.) Boneless chicken breasts
1 teaspoon of salt
1 teaspoon of paprika
½ cup of coconut oil
3 tablespoons of butter
¼ teaspoon of saffron
2 bay leaves
1 (12-oz.) package of peas
½ cup sliced black olives
1 cup of chicken broth

Cook all ingredients together on a stove top EXCEPT bay leaves. Preheat oven to 350 degrees. Line a baking dish with bay leaves. Add in skillet mix and bake for 10 minutes. Add water as needed to prevent chicken from drying out during the baking process.

Serves 6

Americana

Saffron Chicken
Serve with your favorite cooked Vegetable & Salad

Americana

Eggplant Casserole

¼ cup chopped onion
3 chopped garlic cloves
1/3 cup coconut oil
4 red bell peppers, julienne cut
2 ½ cups of sliced zucchini
2 ½ cups peeled and diced eggplant
One 15-oz. can diced tomatoes, with liquid
2 teaspoons of fresh basil
Salt and pepper to taste.

Preheat oven to 350 degrees. In large ovenproof skillet, sauté onion and garlic in coconut oil over medium heat until tender. Add peppers, zucchini, eggplant, tomatoes, and basil. Bake in skillet 30 minutes, uncovered, to reduce liquid. Cover and bake 15 minutes longer. Add salt and pepper.

Lunch & Dinner
Americana

Eggplant Casserole
Serve with your favorite Protein & Salad

Lunch & Dinner
Americana

Lamb Burger over Salad and Cooked Broccoli drizzled with Ranch Dressing.

Weigh out 2-ounce salad including 4-oz onions and Pico de Gallo tomato mix.
Weigh out 6 –ounces of steamed broccoli
Weigh out 4 –oz. of ground lamb and cook in skillet.
Add broccoli to salad and add cooked lamb over broccoli.
Drizzle 1 ½ tables poon of ranch over meal. Enjoy!

Lunch & Dinner
Americana

Lamb Burger over Salad and Cooked Broccoli drizzled with Ranch Dressing.

Tofu and Black Bean Sauce
Serve with 6-oz. salad.

Weigh out 4-oz. of fried tofu and pan fry in 2 tablespoon of Black bean sauce with 1/2 tablespoon of garlic and 3 strands of green onions. Add 6-oz of vegetables (Taste best with sliced yellow squash and chopped red bell peppers)

Tofu and Black Bean Sauce

Lunch & Dinner
Asian

Asian Stir Fry with Zucchini Noodles and Mixed Veggies
Serve with your favorite protein & salad

Cut up 6-ounces of the following veggies weighing your squash or zucchini first. Then, add the following into a skillet on medium high:

-½ a yellow squash or zucchini (shredded like spaghetti noodles)
-cherry tomatoes
-mushrooms
-white onions
-green onions
-red bell pepper

Add 4 ounces of meat. It taste best with fried tofu, chicken, shrimp, or steak for fajitas.

Lunch & Dinner
Asian

Asian Stir Fry with Zucchini Noodles and Mixed Veggies

Asian

Thai Veggie lettuce wraps
Serve with 6-oz. cooked veggies

Break off Large leaves enough to pour over your 4-oz. of meat and your cold veggies.
Weigh out your Green leaves and cold veggies as if it were your 6-oz salad. Separate on plate.

Pour over 4-oz of your favorite meat and cold veggies.

Drizzle your favorite Asian Stir Fry Sauce.

Lunch & Dinner
Asian

Thai Veggie lettuce wraps

Thai Zucchini Noodles with Onions & Shrimp

Serve with a 6-oz. Salad

Weigh out 6-oz of shrimp and cook.

Weigh 6-oz. of a combination of yellow spaghetti squash, green spaghetti zucchini, and white onion. Boil the veggies for 1 minute.

Cook on stove with 1 ½ Tablespoon of Thai green curry paste.

Lunch & Dinner
Asian

Thai Zucchini Noodles with Onions & Shrimp

Egg Drop Soup
Serve with a salad.

4 cups (32 oz.) chicken or vegetable stock
1 tablespoon + 1 teaspoon cornstarch
2 large eggs
Salt or soy sauce

Pour the stock into a saucepan and place over medium-high heat. Put the smaller flavoring extras you're using into a tea ball or spice bag. Add all your flavoring extras to the saucepan with the stock. Turn down the heat to medium-low and simmer for 15 minutes. Scoop out all the flavoring extras with a slotted spoon. Taste and add salt or soy sauce as needed.

Add any soup extras to the stock and simmer for five minutes. Save some scallions for sprinkling on top of the soup at the end.

Scoop out 1/4 cup or so of the stock and whisk it with 1 tablespoon of cornstarch in a small bowl. Whisk this back into the stock and let it simmer for a minute or two until the broth no longer tastes starchy.

Whisk together the eggs in a small bowl with the remaining teaspoon of cornstarch. Make sure your soup is at a bare simmer. Holding a fork over the bowl (see photo), pour the eggs slowly through the tines. Whisk the broth gently with your other hand as you pour. Let the soup stand for a few seconds to finish cooking the eggs.

Serve immediately, topped with thinly sliced scallions.

Serves 4

Egg Drop Soup

Filipino Pork Menudo
Serve with Salad.

2 cups of pork (cut into small chunks)
5 pieces chorizo Bilbao, or sweet italian sausage (also cut in small pieces)
4 potatoes (peeled, cut in small cubes, fried)
1 green bell pepper and 1 red bell pepper (diced)
1 cup chickpeas
1/2 teaspoon paprika
1 cup pork or chicken broth
2 teaspoons of fish sauce
3 tablespoons of oil
3 tomatoes (diced)
1 small head of garlic (minced)
1 medium size onion, diced
1 pc small carrot, medium diced

Cook meat separate from veggies so you can weigh our 4-oz. of meat with each 6-oz. of veggie serving.

*Once you have reached your goal weight serve with 4-oz of rice.

Lunch & Dinner
Asian

Filipino Pork Menudo

Healing Chickpea Soup with Ginger
Serve with 6-oz. salad.

For the Broth:
2 cups of Water
6 cups of chicken stock
1 large onion, chopped
3 stalks celery, chopped
1 large carrot, chopped
1 whole head garlic, cut in half cross-wise
1/4 to 1/2 cup finely chopped fresh ginger (or more!)
2 to 3 thai chilies, chopped or 1 teaspoon crushed red chili flakes
2 cups chopped shiitake mushrooms
1 stalk fresh lemongrass, chopped
cilantro stems
1 teaspoon whole black peppercorns
3 teaspoons Herbamare or sea salt

For the Soup:
1 medium onion, cut into crescent moons
3 to 4 stalks celery, sliced into diagonals
3 carrots, cut into matchsticks
2 to 3 cups sliced shiitake mushrooms
Add a dash of sea salt and freshly ground black pepper to taste

In a separate pan cook 4-oz of chicken and add to soup with each serving.

Lunch & Dinner
Asian

Healing Chickpea Soup with Ginger

Baingan Bharta (Eggplant Curry)
Serve with 6-oz. salad.

1 large eggplant cut in ½
Take a piece of foil and put on baking sheet.
Put eggplant on top of foil and drizzle oil on it.
Set oven for 400 degrees for 30 minutes put the eggplant in to bake.

Heat skillet & spray pan with oil.
Put the following ingredients in the skillet:
1 chopped onion
3-4 garlic cloves minced
1 teaspoon of cumin
1 teaspoon of mustard seed
1 chopped hot pepper
1 teaspoon of coriander
1 teaspoon of turmeric
Dash of salt
1-12-oz can of diced tomatoes

Stir all ingredients around in pan and let cook. While that is cooking scoop the meat out of the eggplant and add to the skillet. Then, add ½ teaspoon of garam masala, and 1 cup of cilantro. Pour everything into a bowl and mix with a hand held blender.

Lunch & Dinner
Indian

Baingan Bharta (Eggplant Curry)

Kodi Vepudu
Serve with Salad.

Chicken pieces - 1lb (Boneless) Cut up into thin strips.
1-Onions
5 small Chilies
1 teaspoon of yogurt
½ teaspoon of Ginger garlic paste
1 teaspoon Chili powder
3 teaspoon of Oil
1 tsp. garam Masala
Ginger - 1 inch piece (finely chopped)
Garlic - 4to 5 cloves (finely chopped)
Few Bay leaves
Dash Coriander (
½ tsp. Turmeric
Dash of Salt

*Cook Chicken separate. After you cook 4-oz of chicken throw into veggie and spice mix but, make sure you weigh out 6-oz of veggies first and put the rest of the veggies in a container for another meal. Store extra chicken separately as well.

Lunch & Dinner
Indian

Kodi Vepudu

Lamb/Hamburger Keema

Serve over a salad.

Combine all ingredients in large pot and cook until meat is done:
2 tablespoons vegetable oil
1 onion, minced
8 ounces ground lamb
8 ounces ground lean beef
Salt and freshly ground pepper, to taste
2 large cloves garlic, minced
2 firm, ripe tomatoes, diced
1 teaspoon ground ginger
1 teaspoon Garam Masala
1 teaspoon minced fresh hot green chilies, or to taste
3 cups frozen peas
1 lemon, juiced, or to taste
2 to 3 tablespoons minced fresh cilantro, or to taste

Lunch & Dinner
Indian

Lamb/Hamburger Keema

Meatless Italian Bean Sausage
Serve with 6-oz of cooked veggies and a Salad

Combine the following in a small pot:
1 can of pinto beans1 tsp. of veggie broth
1 teaspoon of salt
½ tablespoon of fennel seed
*Once ingredients are soft put in a blender and blend.

Add ¼ cup of water. Put all ingredients back onto stove for 10 minutes until mix thickens and you can shape into sausage links. Once mixture is thick fry patties on stove.

Lunch & Dinner
Italian

Meatless Italian Bean Sausage

Cauliflower Pizza
Bake with your favorite 2-oz toppings of veggies and serve with a 6-oz. salad

For best results:

Place 1 pack of cauliflower in food processor.
Scoop out 2 cups of Cauliflower after it has been shredded up in a food processor.
Empty out the rest of the extra cauliflower for a second pizza into Tupperware for another day.
Mix your 2 cups of cauliflower with 2 cups of mozzarella cheese in your food processor.
Add your favorite no sugar added tomato sauce
Add your favorite veggie toppings
Add meatless Italian sausage

Bake for 20-30mintues at 400 degrees

For Weight loss results:

1oz of cheese for crust
2-oz of cauliflower for crust
Use 2oz. of tomato sauce
2 oz. for veggie toppings

Cauliflower Pizza

Lunch & Dinner
Italian

Zucchini or Squash Spaghetti

Serve with 3-oz salad

Cook 4-oz. of hamburger meat.
Cut up 6-oz. of yellow squash spaghetti
Add 3-oz marinara sauce

Zucchini or Squash Spaghetti

Pesto Soup
Serve with Chicken Salad

3 leeks
2 tbsp. of butter
3 garlic cloves cut up
1 tablespoon of fennel seed
2 zucchini
1-oz of green beans
3 medium tomatoes
1 tablespoon of lemon zest
3 tablespoons of fresh basil
4 cups of veggie broth
Add a dash of salt and pepper to taste.

Poor all ingredients into a blender and blend then pour into a large pot and heat on high until warm.

Pesto Soup

Italian Vegetable Soup

Cook 1 pound Italian Sausage or ground beef and weigh it all out into 4-oz servings and set aside.

In a large pot set to high heat and combine the following ingredients:

1 cup of chopped onion
1 cup of celery
1 cup sliced carrots
1 tablespoons of minced garlic
1-15oz of black beans and kidney beans
2 cups of water
5 teaspoons of beef bouillon granules
1 tablespoon of dried parsley flakes
16-oz can of diced tomatoes
15-oz can of tomato sauce
½ teaspoon of dried oregano
½ teaspoon of basil
2 ½ cups of shredded cabbage
dash of salt and pepper

Scoop out 6-oz of vegetables and add 4-oz. of meat and serve.

*Once you hit goal weight you can drizzle some parmesan cheese over each serving.

Lunch & Dinner
Italian

Italian Vegetable Soup

Ratatouille on Squash

Serve with a salad.

Combine all ingredients in a large pot and put on high heat:
1 medium eggplant sliced
1 red bell pepper sliced
1 onion sliced
2 garlic cloves
2 tablespoons of coconut oil
1 yellow squash sliced into spaghetti
1 yellow squash cut up
8-oz. of mushrooms
2 large tomatoes, sliced
1 teaspoon of dried basil
1 teaspoon of oregano
½ teaspoon of salt
½ teaspoon of black pepper
2 oz. of mozzarella cheese with each 6-oz serving

Ratatouille on Squash

Greek Chick pea soup
Serve with Chicken Salad

Put all ingredients into a blender and mix until like soup. Once it is a soup texture heat up over stove.

1 cup dried chickpeas (garbanzo beans) soaked 12-18 hours
1 onion, chopped into pieces about 1/4 inch
1 T + 3 T olive oil (preferably Greek olive oil for this dish)
1 tsp. dried Greek oregano
1 tsp. dried parsley
8 cups water
Add salt to your liking
Add fresh ground black pepper to taste
1/4 cup fresh squeezed lemon juice

Scoop out 6-oz per serving.

Greek Chick pea soup

Mexican Soup

Shred 1 pound of chicken cook and set aside. Add 4-oz of chicken to every 6-oz. of the broth.

The broth:

2-28-oz. cans diced tomatoes
2 dried pasilla peppers seeded and chopped
½ cup a chopped onion
2 minced garlic cloves
6 cups of chicken broth
1 tablespoon of minced fresh epazote
1 tablespoon of lime juice

*After you reached your weightloss goals cut up ½ an avocado and add to your soup with yellow corn tortillas broken up into small pieces.

Mexican Soup

Cuban

Cuban Black Bean Soup

Cook a pound of chorizo sausage and weigh and separate into 4-oz servings. Once soup is done add meat to every 6-oz of soup.

Add the following ingredients to a blender and blend then add to large pot to heat:

1 medium onion, chopped
1 carrot, diced
1 red bell pepper diced
2 tablespoons of minced garlic
1 teaspoon of salt
¼ teaspoon of black pepper
½ teaspoon of ground cumin
4 cups of chicken broth
2 (15-oz. cans) of black beans
½ cup of sherry (sugar free)

Cuban

Cuban Black Bean Soup

Moroccan Vegetable Stew
Serve with a chicken salad

Combine the following ingredients in a large pot and put on stove at high heat:

2 teaspoons olive oil
1 cup diced carrot
1 cup diced yellow onion
2 garlic cloves minced
1 jalapeno pepper
1 ½ cubed gold potato
2 teaspoons ground cumin
1 teaspoons chili powder
½ teaspoon of ground turmeric
1/8 teaspoon of salt
1 (28 oz.) can diced tomatoes
1 (16oz.) can chick peas
½ cup plain Yogurt
½ cup fresh cilantro

Lunch & Dinner
Moroccan

Moroccan Vegetable Stew

Moroccan

Moroccan Chickpea Stew
Serve with a chicken salad

2 tbsp. extra-virgin olive oil
1 large onion, diced
6 cloves garlic, pressed
 2 tsp. ground cinnamon
 1/4 tsp. cayenne pepper
2 tsp. paprika
1 (400g) can of chopped tomatoes
3 (400g) cans chickpeas, drained and rinsed well
40 fl oz./ 2 pints vegetable stock
2 tsp. sugar
Dash of Sea salt
1 Tablespoon of Freshly ground black pepper
5 oz. of package pre-washed baby spinach
 12 sun dried tomatoes, chopped

Directions:- Heat olive oil in a large pot over medium-high heat. Add the onion and sauté until they begin to turn translucent. Add the garlic to the onions. Lower the heat if browning starts to occur. Add the cinnamon, cumin, cayenne and paprika and sauté a minute or so. Add tomatoes, chickpeas, stock and sugar. Season with a couple pinches of salt and 1 tablespoon of fresh pepper. Stir well.

The chickpeas should be slightly covered with liquid. If the level is too low, add some water to bring it just above the chickpeas. Bring the mixture to a simmer, and then lower the heat to low and gently simmer for 45 minutes. Remove the soup from heat. Use a potato masher to mash up some of the chickpeas right in the pot. Stir in the spinach and let it heat through until wilted, just a few minutes. Season again, to taste, with salt and pepper. Serve the soup, and sprinkle the sun dried tomato pieces on the top with a drizzle of their oil if desired.

Moroccan

Moroccan Chickpea Stew

Mediterranean Spiced Lettuce Wraps

Break off Lettuce to serve as taco shells.
Cook 4-oz. lambs per serving with a tbsp. of spiced fish sauce
Use ½ tbsp. of yogurt sauce mix to drizzle over top of wraps.

2 tsp. olive oil
3 cloves garlic, minced
1 lb. ground lamb (I used New Zealand)
1 T. fish sauce
1 tsp. freshly ground black pepper
Pinch ground cinnamon
Pinch ground coriander

1 head iceberg lettuce

Meat Spice Mix
½ cup mint, chopped
½ cup basil, chopped
½ cup parsley, chopped
1 medium cucumber, peeled, seeded and diced
Juice of ½ lime
½ cup pine nuts, toasted

 Yogurt Sauce

¼ cup Greek yogurt
2 tsp. fish sauce
2 tsp. hot sauce
Juice of ½ lime
1 tsp. honey

Remove core from lettuce and separate leaves, rinse and keep chilled until ready to serve.

In a small bowl, combine Greek yogurt, fish sauce, hot sauce, lime juice and honey. Chill until ready to serve.

In a medium bowl, combine the mint, basil, parsley, cucumber and lime juice. Set aside.

In a large skillet, heat olive oil over medium-high heat. Add garlic and sauté for 1 minute, then add lamb, fish sauce, pepper, cinnamon and coriander. Break up the meat and sauté about 5 minutes or until lamb starts to brown and is cooked through.

Divide mixture among lettuce leaves, drizzle with yogurt-sriracha sauce, top with herb-cucumber mixture and sprinkle with pine nuts.

Lunch & Dinner
Mediterranean

Mediterranean Spiced Lettuce Wraps

Mediterranean

Open Face Shawarma

4-oz of cooked roast beef
6-oz of cooked green peppers, red peppers, onions, and
tomatoes, and red pickled peppers.
6-oz of salad
1 ½ tablespoon of garlic sauce

Cook the Roast beef and cooked veggies together with a ½ tablespoon of
coconut oil on stove for 3-4 minutes then pour on top of salad and drizzle
garlic sauce on top.

Mediterranean

Open Face Shawarma

Chicken Chickpea Bake
Serve with a 6-oz. salad

1 tbsp. of coconut oil
2 small packs of thin cut boneless chicken cooked separate from vegetables and weigh and measure out 4-oz. of chicken per 6-oz of cooked veggie mix.

Cooked Veggie Mix:
1 onion chopped
2 garlic cloves
1 can of hick peas
Simmer for 2 minutes

Add 2 sprigs of thyme
½ cup of red wine(sugar free)
1-12-oz can diced tomatoes
½ cup o chicken stock
Simmer for 10 minutes
1 tsp. salt & pepper
½ cup feta
½ tsp. paprika

Bake 1 hour at 400 degrees

Chicken Chickpea Bake

Homemade dressings

Berry Pomegranate & Strawberry Salad Dressing

1 serving:

1 tablespoon of Braggs Berry Pomegranate Vinaigrette
½ tablespoon of Fiordifrutta strawberries fruit spread.

Homemade dressings

Orange Poppy Seed Dressing

Makes 1 cup

1/3 cup of freshly squeezed orange juice
¼ cup sugar free white wine vinegar
3 Tablespoons of sugar free Dijon-style mustard
2 Tablespoons of coconut oil
1 Tablespoons of poppy seeds
Shake all ingredients together and serve 1 ½ tablespoon serving over salad.

Homemade dressings

Asian Stir Fry Sauce

¼ cup of veg. oil
1-garlic clove chopped
Cook for 2 minutes then, stir in the following ingredients:

¼ cup of soy sauce
¼ cup of rice vinegar
2 tsp. Thai Chili Sauce
2 tsp. Sesame Oil
5-oz. bean sprouts
5-oz. shredded carrots
1 Red bell pepper
5 green onions
½ lb. of mushrooms

Suggested Brand Oils & Dressings

Spectrum Natural Organic Balsamic Vinegar of Modena (Made out of Grape Must Only & in the Kroger Nature's Market Section)
The Old Olive Press Company for oils & vinegars.
Vegetti

Marzetti Simply Dressed Dressing & Light (Ranch)
Kenzoil
Bragg's Liquid Aminos (Natural Soy Sauce Alternative)
Bragg's Pomegranate Vinaigrette
Rice Wine for cooking
Sesame Seed Oil
Sitto/s Fattoush Dressing (Hiller's Market)
All Natural LouAna Coconut Oil
Teta Foods Garlic Sauce
Asian Gourmet Black Bean Sauce
Fiordifrutta Strawberry & Wild Strawberries fruit spread

Made in the USA
Middletown, DE
13 July 2017